Preparing
Young
Children
for Science

Preparing Young Children for Science

A Book of Activities

Lois B. Arnold

**illustrations by
Karen E. Pellaton**

SCHOCKEN BOOKS • NEW YORK

First published by Schocken Books 1980

10 9 8 7 6 5 4 3   86 87

Copyright © 1980 by Lois B. Arnold

Library of Congress Cataloging in Publication Data
Arnold, Lois.
  Preparing young children for science.

  Bibliography: p.
  Includes index.
  1. Science – Study and teaching (Elementary)
2. Educational games. I. Title.
LB1585.A74   372.8′3′044   79-26119

Manufactured in the United States of America
ISBN 0-8052-0641-8

Contents

Acknowledgments

Many of the activities in this book have been selected and adapted from those originally developed by the COPES Project at New York University. This Conceptually Oriented Program in Elementary Science, to which I contributed as editor, is centered on some of the major conceptual schemes in science; its development was supported by funds from the Bureau of Research, United States Office of Education. The selection of the activities was based on their inherent interest, easily available materials, and suitability for use at home with a single young child. I wish to acknowledge my indebtness to others associated with the development of the COPES curriculum, particularly Morris Shamos, J. Darrell Barnard, and Janice Cutler.

Introduction

This book is designed to help those who want to teach young children at home, either as a supplement to preschool and early elementary instruction or in place of it. Developing an understanding of science concepts as an outgrowth of enjoyable activities shared with family members can only serve to reinforce and augment learning acquired in the classroom. The activities here are intended for use with children from about four to eight years old, but individual differences in young children may make them useful over a broader age range. In addition, older and younger brothers or sisters may want to "get into the act" – and learn something too! Nor is the book written only for parents. Aunts, uncles, and grandparents may enjoy helping children learn science, especially in those cases where working parents are unable to do so. Any adult caretaker of young children can carry out the activities with them to their educational advantage.

With the increased awareness of the importance of the family as educator comes the need for concrete suggestions for enhancing children's knowledge and capabilities. A problem with many experiences with science at home is that they are not systematic and sustained enough to make a real difference in learning. Typically, a child will do one or more brief "experiments" that are unrelated and that lead nowhere in particular. The selection and arrangement of the activities in this book are meant to circumvent the exclusively hit-or-miss aspect of most such experiences. The fifteen activities are divided into five sets of interrelated experiences. While any one of the fifteen can be done separately, a child will learn more if all three activities in the group are completed in the order in which they are presented. For example, the child can learn a great deal from a walk in the woods, particularly one in which he or she is guided in making observations, but will learn more if the excursion is followed up by examining the woodland "litter" and/ or by making a terrarium, by reading about the plants and animals discovered, and so on. (See Part III.) This way, the child's understanding of natural phenomena can broaden and develop over time.

The role of the parent or other caretaker in these science experiences is an active one. The parent assembles the materials necessary to carry out the activity and guides the child, not only by telling but by asking leading questions and by listening. Examples of such questions are given in the text, and a list of materials that you will need appears at the beginning of each activity. No special knowledge of science is required, nor is it necessary to order any equipment from scientific supply houses. All the materials needed for the activities are either already found in most households or are easily obtainable at drug and hardware stores, grocery stores, and the like. In a few cases, it is suggested that pages in this book be reproduced for the child to use in carrying out the activity. Then just follow the procedure described. Where an activity seemed overlong for the limited attention span of a young child, the procedure has been divided into sections. Some of the activities conclude with Extensions, suggestions for going further and enriching the child's understanding with additional experiences. Enjoy them together.

I

THE
PROPERTIES
OF THINGS

1.

Color, Shape, and Texture

The classification of objects has always been of great importance in science, especially in biology but also in other fields. All the various classification schemes have one function: to impose order on a variety – sometimes an enormous variety – of otherwise disorderly objects and thus to render them more comprehensible. Even very young children can grasp the rudiments of classifying, or grouping things according to their properties. This activity focuses on three properties of objects: color, shape, and texture. By observing and comparing objects that differ in these characteristics, the child will learn that things have more than one property and that these different properties can be used to group them. He will see that any given object may be grouped in different ways, depending on the property he chooses as the basis for grouping. And he will learn to make a record of the different classifications. Record keeping teaches the child that what he observes, and what he does with what he observes, are of value. Records also make it possible to communicate one's findings to others.

MATERIALS

2 pieces of construction paper of contrasting colors (for example, orange and green)
1 piece of sandpaper
3 crayons that match the colors of the papers (for example, orange, green, and the brown color of the sandpaper)
1 pair of shears
1 pair of child's scissors
several sheets of plain white paper, 8½ by 11 inches (21.6 by 27.9 cm)

PROCEDURE

A. Begin by enlisting the child's aid in drawing and cutting out the following shapes from the construction paper and sandpaper:

4 circles, all about 2 inches (5 cm) in diameter: 2 orange and 1 green cut from the construction paper, and 1 brown circle cut from the sandpaper
4 squares, all about 2 inches (5 cm) on a side: 2 orange, 1 green, and 1 brown sandpaper square

You will probably need to cut out the sandpaper circle and square yourself, using the shears. If the child wonders why you are doing all this, tell him you will be using the 8 objects to play a grouping game.

Once the circles and squares are cut out, mix them all up and put them in a pile. Then ask:
• Do these things make a group?
The child will probably answer yes — and he will be right. Merely being together is reason enough to call them a group. For

instance, they can be thought of as a group of colored objects or as a group of paper shapes. Discuss the idea that a group means two or more objects together. A single thing by itself is not a group.

• How could they be put into smaller groups that are alike?

Take some time to discuss this question, too. Give the child a chance to think about it. Typically the child will first suggest color as a basis for grouping objects. That is, he may say that the objects could be divided into three groups: those that are orange, those that are green, and those that are brown. If he does, accept this idea and ask him to arrange the objects into the three groups of different colors on one of the pieces of plain paper. If you want to emphasize the three groups, either you or he could use a pencil to draw a line on the paper between each group.

• Are there any other ways of grouping the objects?

The process of looking for similarities should be well under way by now. If the child first suggested grouping the objects by color, he may now indicate that they could also be grouped according to their shape. Using this property, there would be two groups, one containing the four circles and the other containing the four squares. As soon as he suggests this, let him rearrange the objects into the two groups of different shape. Again, a line could be drawn between the groups on the paper.

Another basis for grouping is texture: Some of the shapes are rough and some are smooth. The two rough objects both happen to be brown, but this is irrelevant for purposes of a classification based on texture, just as it is irrelevant that the six smooth objects are orange and green. Don't confuse the child by trying to have him deal with classifications based on more than one property at once. Most young children can deal with only one variable at a time, and then only with the actual concrete objects in front of them. Also, don't expect him to come up with the word "texture"; he probably won't. Instead, let him express the basis for his groupings in his own words, and then you can tell him that the name of that property is texture. Let him try pronouncing the word. Then he can arrange the objects into rough and smooth groups on the paper.

So far, the child should have come to realize that objects have more than one property. Another way of saying this is that a combination of properties is necessary to describe or define a given object. The child should also understand that these properties, such as shape, color, and texture, can be used to classify or group objects. Notice that whatever the basis of the classification scheme, it is a matter of human choice. This is why it is important for children to have the experience of looking for similarities in the properties of objects and then of grouping them according to the one(s) they select. There is no single "right way" to classify things.

B. After the child has grouped the 8 objects in various ways on the basis of their properties, suggest making a record of the groupings. It is important for children to learn to keep track of what they do. You might start with the last grouping the child made. If he had just recently arranged the objects into rough and smooth groups, ask:

• How could you make a picture of these groups?

Explain to the child that if he made a picture of the classification, he could use it to show others how he grouped the objects. One of the important functions of records is to communicate one's findings. Here is another way of getting at this: Substituting a known distant relative for the one below, ask:

• Suppose you wanted to show Aunt Nellie how you grouped these things. How would you do it?

However you choose to focus the child's attention on record keeping, be prepared to accept a variety of responses. There are many ways of making a record of the various groupings. However, in guiding him, you should be aware of certain pitfalls and opportunities. For example, suppose he suggests making a record of his groupings based on texture by pasting down the objects that he has arranged into the two groups on the paper. This would certainly provide a permanent record of

TEXTURE

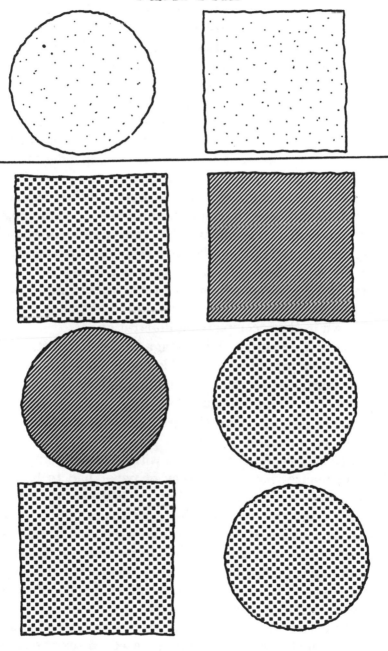

that particular classification. But then he would not be able to use the same objects to record his groupings according to color and shape. A better solution would be to outline the objects in their positions on the paper, remove them, and then color in the outlined figures, which will *represent* the objects. The crayons can be used to color in the figures so that they match the objects. Thus he can make a picture of the classification that is separate from the objects themselves. In this method of record keeping, there is a one-to-one correspondence between the objects and their representations on the paper. They are virtually identical (except for texture). The child should have no trouble in seeing the connection between the groupings and the record of the groupings. He can proceed to record the groupings based on the other two properties in a similar manner. He will end up with three separate record sheets—one for color, one for shape, and one for texture, with pictures of the various groupings on them. A sample record sheet for texture is shown in the accompanying illustration.

Depending on the child's stage of development, you may be able to go further with record keeping. For instance, instead of tracing the paper shapes, he could draw similar but smaller figures. Try asking this question:

• How could you record the groupings for color, shape, and texture on one piece of paper?

See if the child can come up with a way of doing this. He should realize that three pieces of paper had to be used to record the groupings in the first method because the traced figures that represent the objects are the same size as the objects themselves. If a small square were used to represent a bigger square, and a small circle to represent a bigger circle, the groupings could be shown in a smaller amount of space. This would be a better method of record keeping because it's more economical—it saves paper.

An even more economical procedure would be to use symbols. For instance, the groupings based on texture shown in the illustration could be represented using the letters R and S

to stand for "rough" and "smooth." There are 2 R's and 6 S's. But in this scheme there is no visual resemblance between the representation of the groupings and the actual groupings of the objects, and many young children are not ready to handle this degree of abstraction. Take the child only as far along this road as he can go.

2.
Magnetic Properties

Objects have many properties other than color, shape, and texture. Some of these properties cannot be seen or felt. For example, some things respond to the pull of a magnet and others do not. It isn't possible to tell which are magnetic simply by looking at them or feeling them. Magnetism is a kind of hidden property. This activity is designed to reinforce what the child has learned about classifying objects, by providing additional experience with grouping on the basis of properties, and to introduce a new property: magnetism. He will find that some metallic objects are pulled toward, or attracted by, a magnet and some are not. Thus this magnetic force can be used to discriminate among things that are made of metal.

MATERIALS

1 magnet
several small objects, some magnetic and some not, such as: paper clips, scraps of paper, iron nails, thumbtacks, pieces of string or yarn, rubber bands, brass tacks, pieces of copper wire, bits of aluminum foil

PROCEDURE

Show the child the group of objects you have assembled, but don't bring out the magnet yet.

• How could you group these objects?

Let him suggest the properties he might use to group them. It may not occur to him right away that they could be grouped into things that are made of metal and things that are not. Since he just worked with the property of color, the child may want to discriminate among them on this basis – the brass tacks are yellow, the thumbtacks are red, the yarn is blue, etc. Or he might put all the pointed or hard things, like tacks and nails, in one pile and everything else in another. This is perfectly acceptable. The property of hardness, or resistance to scratching, is often used by geologists to tell one mineral from another. It is a useful property to know about.

After the child has had a chance to observe the objects and divide them up on the basis of the properties he has chosen, bring out the magnet. Ask if he knows what it is. If he doesn't, explain that it is an object that has magnetic force – it can pull certain other objects toward itself. If the child asks what a force is, remind him that he himself uses force whenever he pulls or pushes things. Then suggest that he try and see if any of the objects might be drawn to the magnet.

• What kinds of objects are attracted by the magnet?

If the child says that metals are pulled by the magnet, point out that the aluminum foil, the brass tacks, and the copper wire are made of metal but are not attracted to it. (Brass is a mixture of copper and zinc.) Only some kinds of metallic objects – such as thumbtacks, iron nails, and paper clips – respond to the magnetic force. All of these objects contain the metal iron, either by itself or in the form of steel. One of the properties of the metal iron is that it is attracted by a magnet.

• How could you group the objects on the basis of this property?

Of course, the child could simply divide them up into two groups: those that are pulled or attracted to the magnet and those that are not. But he could also further subdivide the nonmagnetic group into metals and nonmetals. Here again, there is no single correct way of classifying the objects. However, when the child has made his groupings, encourage him to record the classification scheme by making a picture or drawing of it as he did in the previous activity.

Extension

Taste is another property that children enjoy investigating. As with magnetism, it is not possible to detect this property simply by looking at an object. Exploring the property of taste can help children move away from depending exclusively on the sense of sight to identify or group objects. It will help reinforce the idea that there may be many different properties that can be used in classification.

Prepare three different solutions ahead of time: Put a few ounces of water into each of three small, clear glasses or cups of the same size, and add about ½ teaspoon of salt to one cup and ½ teaspoon of sugar to the second. Stir until both are dissolved. To the third glass, add about 1 teaspoon of strained lemon juice. You will then have three solutions which look very much the same. The child may try smelling them, which is fine – odor is another related property of objects. Then suggest that he take a sip of one. How does it taste? Have him rinse out his mouth with water and sip the next. After tasting all three solutions, he should realize that even though they all look alike, one is salty, one is sweet, and one is sour.

If you wish, ask the child to classify a selected group of foods that are predominantly salty, sweet, or sour on the basis of their taste. Later on, in activity 13, the child will have an opportunity to investigate hidden patterns in the property of taste.

3.

Germination Time

Germination is a property of seeds. Within this general category of objects, different kinds of seeds take different amounts of time to germinate. In other words, seeds can be classified not only on the basis of such obvious properties as color, shape, and size, but also on the basis of another, "hidden" property — one that can only be observed over time. If you garden at home, you are probably aware that germination time is given on seed packets. Young children are generally not aware of this and may not even have had the opportunity to observe the process of germination, which usually goes on under ground. In this activity the child will be able to observe the germination of different kinds of seeds and keep a record of the number that sprout on each of three successive days. Counting the seeds before and after they sprout will not only help him keep track of what happens and make meaningful comparisons among the seed types possible, but will also help prepare him for the next set of activities, on measurement.

This is a nice activity to do in the spring, when seeds are easily obtainable; otherwise, you can use red kidney and lima beans, which are available at the grocery store all year round. If you are planning to plant a family garden and have other types of seeds on hand, you might add a few other kinds for your child to observe. Seeds differ widely in their external appearance, coming in a variety of sizes, shapes, and colors, and this could provide a good opportunity to introduce him to classification in living things.

Radish seeds are suggested for this activity because they germinate very rapidly — usually within 24 hours. Red kidney beans can be expected to sprout within 24 to 48 hours and lima beans within 48 to 72 hours. Other kinds of seeds with different germination times can be substituted for these, but avoid those that take several days to sprout because under these growing conditions such seeds are likely to become moldy before germinating.

MATERIALS

3 different kinds of seeds such as radish seeds, red kidney beans, and lima beans
3 plates or other flat dishes
3 or more paper towels
1 pair of tweezers (optional)
3 clear plastic food-storage bags and ties
plain paper

PROCEDURE

A. Put several of each of the three different kinds of seeds in separate piles on a sheet of paper and ask:
• What are these things?

After establishing that the objects are seeds and that seeds can grow into plants, ask:
• How could you classify the seeds?

By now, the child should know that "classifying" is another word for grouping objects according to their properties. Let him tell you how he would go about grouping them. He will probably suggest arranging them on the basis of their color, shape, or size. This is fine. It is not necessary to actually do a classification. Indeed, it wouldn't make much sense if you have only three types of seeds. But do discuss the possibilities with him.

Next, tell the child that another property of living seeds is that they can germinate, or start to grow. Suggest that it would be fun to see how long it would take for these seeds to germinate. To do this, you will not plant the seeds in the ground outside or under the soil in a pot. Instead, you will start them growing in a way that enables you both to watch them sprout.

• What do seeds need in order to start growing?

Before setting up the germinating dishes, be sure the child understands that the seeds will need water in order to sprout. Light, however, is not necessary for germination. In fact, direct sunlight is not conducive to seed growth.

Bring out the three plates or other flat dishes and enlist the child's aid in preparing the germinators. First fold the paper towels to fit the bottom of the dishes. Then wet the towels. Put the same amount of water on each one. The towels should not be dripping wet – just moist. Next, the child can count out the same number of seeds of each kind and put them in their respective dishes. For example, he could put 10 radish seeds in one dish, 10 red kidney beans in the second dish, and 10 lima beans in the third dish. Because the beans are large, you might need to use a larger dish or two dishes for them. Don't use too few seeds, because not all of them will germinate – as the child should discover. Don't use too many seeds either. When the dishes are ready, slip a clear plastic food-storage bag over each one and tie it loosely. This will retard evaporation of the water and prevent the seeds from drying out.

Note that the instructions call for the same number of seeds of each kind and the same amount of water on each paper towel. Similarly, the child should check the dishes for any sprouted seeds at the same time each day. There is a reason for holding these factors constant. Heat and light should be kept constant too. If you wish to establish that different

kinds of seeds take different and characteristic amounts of time to germinate, it is important to eliminate other factors that might affect the germination times. For instance, suppose the seeds in dish 2 sprouted before the seeds in dish 1, but dish 2 had received more water than dish 1; then it would be reasonable to argue that the seeds in dish 2 germinated earlier because they had more water. However, young children are usually incapable of understanding the reasoning behind this. It doesn't bother them at all if there is twice as much water in one dish as another. The best approach to this problem is simply to direct the child in setting up the germinators so that it will be possible to make meaningful comparisons of germination times without elaborate or confusing explanations. Seeing that this activity is done the right way will help the child get into the habit of careful, systematic experimentation.

B. If you set up the germinating dishes in the evening, the child should be encouraged to observe the seeds over the course of the next day without disturbing them.
• What changes do you notice in the seeds?
   He may notice that some of the seeds have swelled. Eventually the seed coats will split and root tips appear.
• How will we know when the seeds have germinated?
   It is necessary to establish a criterion for germination. Seeds that are not viable may swell simply through the ab-

sorption of water. Thus swelling, or even splitting of the seed coat, is not necessarily a sign that the seed will grow. But when the root tip appears, the seed is starting to grow.

By the next evening, some of the radish seeds will probably have germinated – that is, some of their root tips will have appeared, perhaps nearly all. At this point, the plastic bag should be opened and the child should count how many have germinated. As they are counted, they can be removed from the dish. It may be easier to grasp the small radish seeds with tweezers. The number of germinations should be recorded on a sheet of paper set up like the one illustrated here.

Number of Seeds _____			
Day/Time	Number of Germinations		
	Dish 1	Dish 2	Dish 3

Removing the germinated seeds makes it easier to see the others as they germinate on successive days. By the evenings of the second and third days, the bean seeds should have begun to sprout, and they can be counted. By the fourth day, all the seeds that are going to germinate will have done so. It should be clear that each of the different kinds of seeds takes a different amount of time to sprout, the radish seeds taking the least and the lima beans the most time. Germination time is a property that can be used to identify the kind of seed. Even seeds that look very much alike may have very different germination times and develop into very different plants.

The method of germination used here is very similar to the ones used to make bean sprouts for eating. Alfalfa, mung, and other seeds are sold commercially for this purpose, and when sprouted they are crunchy and nutritious. Unlike seeds sold for planting, they are not treated with a substance which retards the growth of mold during germination in soil. Do not let the child eat sprouts from seeds treated with mold retardant. However, he may want to plant a few of the sprouts he has germinated in order to observe their subsequent growth. He can plant them in pots indoors, or outdoors if the season and circumstances permit.

II
MEASURING

4.
Put Them in Order

Measurement is fundamental to science. Just as objects have different properties that can be described and compared in qualitative terms, they may also differ in quantifiable properties. For example, things may differ in color, but they may also differ in their linear dimensions — height, width, and length. In order to make comparisons between objects and to recognize when changes occur, it is necessary to measure them. This activity gives the child the experience of comparing objects with respect to their dimensions. It also introduces the concept of serial ordering: The objects are put in order from shortest to longest and from smallest to biggest. The youngest children need this experience before proceeding with measurement.

MATERIALS

- 6 drinking straws, each cut to a different length, but identical in other respects
- 4 to 6 cubes, each a different size, with the smallest about the size of a die (the cubes should sink in water and not dissolve in it, because they will be used in displacement activities later on; they can be made of modeling clay)
- 4 to 6 spheres, each a different size (marbles, golf balls, and the like can be used)

PROCEDURE

Put two of the straws side by side on a table or other flat surface. Be sure the bottom edges of the straws line up.
- How are the two straws alike?
- How are they different?

The child will probably tell you that the shape, color, and other features of the straws are alike but that one is shorter (or longer) than the other. Bring out another straw and ask her which one is the shortest (or longest). Then ask her to put them in order from longest to shortest. Again, be sure the bottom edges of the straws line up, to make the comparison meaningful and easier.

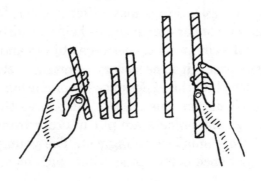

Bring out the remaining three straws. Add them to the rest but do not put them in order. Instead, ask the child to do this. She should be able to arrange all six straws in descending or ascending order of length. Then ask her which is the shortest and which is the longest in length. Using the term "length" will help her keep track of the property that is being compared. This is especially important because "longer" and "shorter" can also refer to time.

Once the child has succeeded in ordering the group of straws into a series showing gradations in length, see if she can apply her understanding of the concept to a new situation. Bring out all the cubes.

• How are the cubes different?

In her own words, she should be able to tell you that the cubes differ in size — some are bigger or smaller than others.

• Which cube is the biggest? Which is the smallest?

After she points out the biggest and smallest cubes, ask her to arrange them in order to size. If she is very young and has trouble doing this, first review the exercise with the straws. Then, after she has put the cubes in order, ask her to order a set of spheres of different sizes. Even if she ordered the cubes quickly and easily, the spheres can be used to reinforce the idea.

Before finishing with the cubes, see if the child can comprehend that the sides of a given cube are all the same length, but the sides of all the cubes differ in length. When all the cubes are in ascending order on the table, ask the child to compare their heights. If necessary, point out that a bigger cube has longer sides than a smaller cube, with the result that the bigger cube takes up more space overall. (Another way of saying this is that the bigger cube has a greater volume than the smaller cube. The child will measure the volume of these cubes in activity 6.)

5.
How Long Is It?

To say that one object is longer or shorter than another tells something about their relative lengths, but sometimes more information is needed. How much longer is one than the other? To answer this question, it is necessary to measure the lengths of the two objects. Such measurement also involves comparison: The length of each object must be compared with that of a measuring instrument which is divided into standard units of length. In this activity the child will make her own ruler to measure the length of various things. In the process, she will be introduced to the idea of a standard unit of measurement and will see that measuring involves counting the number of standard units that "fit" the unknown dimension. She will also see that there are many different standards of length. A suitable standard must be *chosen*, depending on the size of the thing being measured.

MATERIALS

1 piece of string, 1 foot (30 cm) long
1 sheet of paper for recording measurements
1 sheet of plain white paper that can be easily folded
1 strip of cardboard to serve as a backing for the child's ruler
1 pair of scissors

paste

1 ruler, marked in both inches and centimeters

1 thick book, such as a dictionary or metropolitan telephone directory

PROCEDURE

A. Choose a room, such as the kitchen or the child's bedroom, and tell the child you are going to try to find out how long the room is. Starting with your heel lined up at one end, walk across the room, heel to toe, heel to toe, until you come to the other side. Have her count the steps as you go.

• How long is the room in Mommy-feet (or Daddy-feet)?

Perhaps the child counted a total of 12 steps that it took to cover the length of the room. Then it can be said that the room is 12 Mommy-feet long. Record this measurement on a sheet of paper.

By now, the child will probably want to try this herself. Let her do so, counting as she goes. Be sure she places her feet heel to toe each time. Then, substituting the child's name for the one below, ask:

• How long is the room in Susie-feet?

Perhaps the room will measure 20 Susie-feet long. Have the child record this value on the paper also. Which is the correct length? Both are correct! The reason for the difference is that the units of measurement — your foot and her foot — are of different lengths. It takes more shorter units to cover the

same distance. The values obtained for the length of the room would also vary depending on other factors, such as whether the measurements were made in bare feet or with shoes on.

• Suppose Aunt Nellie wanted to know how many feet long your room was. What would you tell her?

This question can help direct the child's attention to the need for a *standard* unit of measurement. A standard is always the same and is agreed upon and understood by everyone. One problem with a "Susie-foot" as a unit of length is that it varies. Ask the child what she thinks will happen to the "Susie-foot" as she gets older. Also, even in an individual adult, the right foot and left foot are not the same length. This is why people take measurements in standard units of length.

Bring out the foot-long piece of string. Tell the child that this length is a standard foot. If she measures her room with this standard, Aunt Nellie and other people would be able to understand how long it is. Help the child use the string to make the measurement: Starting at the end of the room, place the string down so it is stretched to its full length. Have her place her finger at the end of the string. Then lift it up and place the end of the string next to her finger. Repeat this process, counting the feet as you go, until you have covered the distance. This is exactly equivalent to the heel-to-toe procedure.

When you get to the other end of the room, you will probably find that the length does not come out to an exact number of feet. How is such a length to be expressed? Instead of getting involved in confusing explanations of how feet are divided up into inches – after all, the string is not so divided, and that is what the child has in front of her – encourage her to express the length in terms of "more than" and "less than" or "longer than" and "shorter than." It is entirely legitimate for the child to say, for example, that the room is longer than 9 feet but shorter than 10 feet. Or she could say the room is between 9 and 10 feet long. She could also express the measurement to the nearest whole number of feet. Every measurement represents an approximation of some sort with respect to some standard.

B. Now bring out the thick book and show it to the child.
• How could we measure the thickness of this book?

Point out the dimension in question. Ask if she thinks it would be possible to measure the thickness of the book with the foot-long piece of string. Hold the string next to the book for comparison. It should be obvious that the piece of string is too long a standard to be useful in measuring the thickness of the book. All that could be said is that the thickness is less than 1 foot. What is needed is a shorter unit of length.

Suggest that the child try making a ruler that could be used to measure the thickness of the book. Give her a strip of paper about 1½ inches wide and 10 or 11 inches long (4 cm by 25–28 cm). Ask her to fold the strip in half crosswise and, before opening it, predict how many parts there will be. Have

her fold the strip in half again. How many smaller units will there be this time? She should fold the strip in half four times in all, each time predicting how many smaller units will be produced. Making such predictions helps to focus her attention and develops expectations. She will probably predict that the first fold will produce 2 units and the second will produce 4 units. However, she may expect that three folds will produce 6 units. Of course, they don't – the third fold produces 8 units. Similarly, she may not expect the fourth and final fold to produce 16 units.

Next, unfold the paper strip and draw a line partway across it wherever there is a fold. Now the child has a linear measuring device divided into several equal parts. Each of the parts is a unit of length that is repeated across the strip for ease in counting. Have her finish the ruler by cutting the strip off at the end of the *tenth* unit and pasting the 10-unit strip of paper to a strip of cardboard of the same size. This will make a rigid ruler, which lasts longer and reduces the possibility that the child will measure with a strip that is not entirely unfolded and flat. Having the larger unit divided into 10 smaller units prepares her for work with the metric system, in which all the units are multiples of 10 subunits. For example, there are 10 millimeters (mm) in 1 centimeter (cm). On her measuring instrument, the child may want to number the fold lines from 1 to 10, starting to the left of the first fold.

With her ruler, the child can now measure the thickness of the book. Be sure that she lines up the bottom of the ruler with the bottom of the book. As with the straws, to make meaningful comparisons of length, both objects have to start at the same point. As with the length of the room, the measurement can be expressed as an approximation. For instance, the book might be more than 3 units thick and less than 4 units. Encourage the child to practice by measuring other suitable objects as well, recording their dimensions on the record sheet.

• Suppose we measured the length of the room with your ruler. What do you think we'd get?

Give her time to think about this. Of course, she would get a larger number for the length than that obtained previously, because the units on her ruler are smaller than feet. Help her to measure the length of the room with her ruler if she's interested. Just be sure to mark where the end of the ruler falls each time before it is picked up and put down again. See if she can count by tens to come up with a total as you go across the floor. Notice that the value for the length of the room obtained with her ruler is a finer approximation of the actual length than could be made with the string.

Conclude this activity by showing the child the ruler that is marked in inches and centimeters. Point out that this ruler has units just as her ruler does – only these units are standard units of length that many people use. The metric units are understood all over the world.

6.

How Much Is There?

This activity extends the operations of measurement from determining the linear dimensions of an object to determining its volume, or the amount of space it occupies. As in the previous activity, once the unit of measure is selected, it is necessary to count how many of these units "fit into" the object in question. In measuring the length of a room, the number of units of length that cover the distance were counted; similarly, in measuring the volume of a container, the number of unit measures of volume that fill the container are counted. Here, the child will find the volume of two different-size jars using a 1-ounce cup as a unit of volume. Next she will use this unit to prepare scales on the jars to measure multiple volumes. She then uses the jars to find the volume of the cubes introduced in activity 4.

MATERIALS

1 1-ounce (aproximately 30 ml) plastic or wax paper cup, for use as a unit measure of volume. (These are often sold in drug stores as dispensers of liquid medicine. An alternative is a coffee scoop, which holds ⅛ cup, or 1 ounce.)

1 6- to 8-ounce (180 to 240 ml) clear, straight-sided jar, such as an olive jar

1 8- to 12-ounce (240 to 350 ml) clear, straight-sided jar
1 glass-marking pencil, or masking tape and a regular
  pencil
water
food coloring (optional)
a pourable solid, such as sand or cereal
4 to 6 cubes (from activity 4)
1 sheet of paper for recording measurements

PROCEDURE

A. Set up a work place near a source of water in the kitchen or
bathroom – or outdoors if the weather permits – where spills
can be tolerated. Bring out the two clear, straight-sided jars
and show them to the child.
• Which jar do you think will hold more water?
• How could we find out how much more the larger jar holds?
    Expect a quick answer to the first question and a slower
answer to the second. After the child has had time to think
about it, bring out the small 1-ounce cup and say something
like "Let's see how many of these cups of water the smaller jar
will hold." Ask her to fill the small cup to the brim and pour it
into the jar. (Filling to the brim is more accurate and easier
than trying to fill the cup to the same line each time. If you are
using a coffee scoop, there are no lines anyway.) Explain that
the filled cup represents one unit measure of volume. Have her
continue to add cupfuls of water, counting them as they go in.
Don't rush. Make it seem important that she do this carefully.
When the jar is almost full, the child may find that the next
cupful of water overflows it. That is, the jar may not hold exactly 6 or 8 ounces. If it doesn't, point out how this is like
measuring the length of the room or the thickness of the book:
The volume of the jar is between two values. It might hold
more than 7 ounces but less than 8. Whatever the final
measurement, it should be recorded on a sheet of paper.

This same procedure should be followed to find the volume of the larger jar in unit measures. The number of cupfuls it takes to fill this jar should also be recorded on the sheet of paper. Then it will be possible to answer the original question. The child should be able to see that if the smaller jar holds 6 unit measures, say, and the larger jar holds 8 unit measures, the larger jar holds 2 more measures than the smaller one. Measuring the volume of both jars has made it possible to say how much more one holds than the other.

B. Point out that it takes a lot of time to find the volume of a container by repeatedly pouring in unit measures, one at a time. Sometimes you lose count, too. It would be useful to have a measuring device on which the number of unit measures could simply be read off — just as the child could read off different lengths on her ruler. Suggest to her that you try making such a device, using the larger jar.

• How could we use the unit measuring cup to make a measuring device out of the jar?

The child may have noticed earlier how the level of water in the jar went up each time she added a unit measure of water. If those levels could be marked on the jar somehow, she would have such a device. It is difficult to mark glass directly, though. It takes a special glass-marking pencil to do it. Such pencils are available at art supply stores, but it is not necessary to buy one. If you have some masking tape at home, press a narrow strip vertically along the side of the jar. The water levels can be marked on the masking tape with a regular pencil.

Once you have settled on a way of marking water levels on the large jar, ask the child to pour in the first unit measure cup of water. She should then mark the level while viewing the liquid height at eye level. (When the device is completed, it should also be read at eye level to minimize error. Coloring the water with a few drops of food coloring makes it easier to read the level.) The mark should be put right on the edge of the tape, if that method is being used. Then the next cupful should be poured in, the second mark put on the tape, and so on, until the scale is completed. Because the sides of the jar are straight, the markings on the scale should be the same distance apart. She may want to put numbers next to the markings.

Now the child has a device that can easily be used to measure volumes smaller than that of the jar.

• Suppose we filled the smaller jar with water and poured it into the larger jar. How far up would the water come?

See if she can answer this question. If she can't, don't answer it yourself. Instead, have her try it. If she found that the smaller jar contained 6 unit measures of water originally, she should find that the water level comes up to the sixth mark from the bottom when she pours this amount into the larger jar.

Children enjoy using their measuring devices to find the volume of various containers. Try asking the child to find the volume of a small juice glass. She should fill it to the brim, pour it into the marked jar, and read the water level. It is easiest to read the level to the nearest whole unit of volume. The number can then be recorded.

When the child has had some practice with her measuring

device, you might bring out a pint jar and ask her how she could find out how many unit measures it contains using the device. Since there are 16 ounces in a pint, this will be a challenging problem; the marked jar will not hold that amount of water. This is similar to the earlier problem of measuring a length that was longer than the ruler. One way of solving it is by filling the pint jar with water and pouring the water into the measuring device a few ounces at a time. For instance, the child could fill the device up to the sixth mark from the bottom, empty the water out, and then fill it up to the sixth mark again and empty it again. She should record the amounts each time, thus preparing to add them up. In this case, when she pours the remainder of the water from the pint jar into the device, the water should come up to the fourth mark from the bottom because 6 ounces plus 6 ounces plus 4 ounces add up to 16 ounces, or 16 unit measures.

C. Begin this section by asking the child if she thinks it would be possible to use the measuring device to find the volume of solids. Don't hesitate to use the word "volume" with her. It refers to the amount of space something takes up and is not a particularly difficult word. On the other hand, it is the understanding that is most important. For instance, the process of putting a scale on a measuring device is called calibrating the instrument. It is more important that she understand what is involved in the process, and why it is a necessary part of measurement, than that she use the word "calibrate." However, hearing such words used correctly in the ordinary course of conversation helps children increase their vocabulary. Often they enjoy using "big words."

Pour some sand, fine-grained cereal, or other pourable solid into a dish and show it to her.

• How much is there?

The sand or cereal can be poured into the calibrated jar and its volume measured just as a liquid's can. Have her try it.

Now bring out the cubes that were introduced in activity

4. Choose a cube that will fit into the mouth of the calibrated jar and that will raise the water level by at least one unit measure. Fill the jar with water to one of the markings about halfway up.

• What do you think will happen to the water if I drop this cube into it?

The child should be able to predict that the water level will rise. Drop the cube in and then discuss with her what the rise in water level means: The level rises because the cube takes up some of the space that was occupied by water. This water that was "pushed out of the way," or displaced, by the cube has to go somewhere, and the result is that the water level rises by an amount equal to the volume of the cube. This fact makes it possible to measure the volume of solids that are not in the form of small, pourable particles. Here are the steps involved in finding the volume of a solid object by the water displacement method:

1. Record the water level before the object is put into the calibrated jar. If you don't know what the level was to start with, it won't be possible to find out how much it has risen.
2. Put the object into the water. Of course, don't use an object that is soluble in water. For instance, you can't find the volume of a sugar cube by this method! Also, the object must be totally submerged. Otherwise, the rise in the water level will not be equivalent to the total volume of the object.
3. Record the water level again.
4. Subtract the first water level reading from the second. Their difference tells how much space the object takes up. If the original level of water in the jar was 2 unit measures, and it rose to 5 unit measures when the cube was submerged, the volume of the cube is 3 unit measures.

Encourage the child to find the volumes of the remaining cubes, after you have guided her through the method once. There are two challenging problems that may arise while she is doing this. First, she may find that one of the cubes is too big to fit into her calibrated jar. How can the volume of this cube be found? One way would be to get a larger jar – one that the cube will fit into – and calibrate it. If the jar is wide and the markings turn out to be too close together, mark every 2 unit measures – or even every 5 – instead of every 1. This larger device can then be used to find the volume of the larger cube.

Second, she may find that the smallest cube will not raise the water level enough to be measurable. How can the volume of this cube be found? She might want to try calibrating the smaller of the two jars she used originally and see if that would work. However, she still may not be able to get a large enough change in the water level. See if she realizes that it may be necessary to use a smaller unit of volume. If she does, you can congratulate yourself. She has really learned something! She could take a small jar and use a tablespoon as a unit measure – or even a thimble – to make a scale. Problems like this should be regarded as teaching opportunities.

III

ECOLOGY
AND
ENVIRONMENT

7.

A Walk
in the Woods

This activity is both a necessary and a desirable precursor to activities 8 and 9, in which the child will examine natural woodland "litter" and build a terrarium. Before those activities can be undertaken, you should take the child to a wooded area where he can explore and collect the material he will need. This trip can be turned into an enjoyable family outing.

If you have done some of the preceding activities with the child, he will have become sensitive to the different properties and characteristics of the things he sees on the trip and will be able to make meaningful comparisons among them. He should be aware of the color, shape, and texture of things in nature and also of their different dimensions. He should be prepared to observe, to record, and to look for changes in organisms and their environment. Naturalists are made, not born.

MATERIALS

1 child's shovel or garden trowel
1 large plastic bag, approximately 1 gallon capacity
1 large, sturdy cardboard box, for bringing back stones, pieces of wood, plants, and other large objects for the terrarium.
1 hardcover notebook containing plain, unlined paper, and a pencil
camera (optional)

PROCEDURE

First you must locate a suitable wooded area for exploration and collecting. This can be tricky, especially if you live in a city. The wooded region need not be large, but it should be sufficiently "wild" so that you will be able to collect a limited amount of renewable material without permanently disturbing the environment. Avoid places such as nature preserves and wildflower or bird sanctuaries. For good reason, such places usually have strict rules against taking anything out. A designated wilderness area is ideal, but there are few of these in the United States, and it will probably be necessary to settle for a state or city park that contains wooded sections. Even in the nation's largest city, New York, there is such a park within the city limits and reachable by subway and bus: Van Cortlandt Park. For New Yorkers, this park would be a better choice than the more heavily used and carefully planted Central Park.

Once you have located a suitable woodland area for exploration, prepare the child for this "field trip" by going to the library and looking up books about the woods. Children's librarians can be particularly helpful in recommending such books. One good one is *Into the Woods: Exploring the Forest Ecosystem* by Laurence Pringle, which is illustrated with photographs. Another is *In Woods and Fields* by Margaret Waring Buck. It is unfortunately out of print but available in libraries. A helpful feature of this book is that it's divided up by seasons. *A Walk in the Forest: The Woodlands of North America* by Albert and Ilka List is also excellent, but better suited to older children.

With city children, it is nice to start by familiarizing them with their own natural surroundings. Here again, books can be helpful in heightening their awareness – for example, *Wild Green Things in the City: A Book of Weeds* by Anne Ophelia

Dowden and *City Rocks City Blocks and the Moon* by Edward Gallob, about fossiliferous building stones and other evidence of geology in the city. Another book by Gallob that can be recommended is *City Leaves, City Trees.*

If you live in an area of the country where the ground is frozen in the winter months, don't plan to go on your collecting trip at that time. Wait until the late spring, summer, or early fall. The insects and other organisms you want to collect in the woodland litter on the forest floor are not active in cold weather. Plants are dormant and many animals are in hibernation. However, you might like to visit the wooded area in the winter to observe and perhaps to take photographs for later comparison. In deciduous forests, the trees are bare in winter, so there is much more light for picture taking. Such a visit will help to make a child aware of seasonal changes in the environment. A book like *Winter Buds* by Bette J. Davis would add to the experience.

Set out on a warm day soon after a rain. Sensible, walking shoes are essential, and long pants are advisable, to help prevent scratches and insect bites. Many people find an insect repellent helpful. You may find yourself walking through a field or meadow to get to the woods, but don't plan too long a hike. You'll be twice as tired by the time you've walked back carrying material.

Having arrived at a suitable spot in the woods, stop and look around. Look up at the canopy of trees overhead. Sit down and listen to the sounds. Watch for movements. This would be a good time for the child to make a drawing in the notebook of what he sees, since the light may be too dim here to take photographs without special attachments. He will need to record the general appearance of the environment — for example, whether it is hilly or flat — since he will be re-creating it in a terrarium in activity 9.

Next look down where there are decaying leaves, pieces of rotting wood, and other such woodland litter. Fill the plastic bag with the litter, digging up the layers carefully with the small shovel or trowel. Don't permit the child to pick up handfuls and throw them into the bag. Instead, ask him to dig around the area to a depth of at least 4 inches and carefully lift the litter out without disturbing the layers any more than necessary. The natural litter on the floor of the woods constitutes an ecological niche with its own characteristic assemblage of organisms. This organic material will be loose and there may be a few low plants growing in it. You will also see some insects and other creatures in it. If it has recently rained, the litter will be moist. If it seems dry, sprinkle the contents of the bag with water when you get home. It should be stored away from light and extreme changes in temperature.

Before leaving the woodland area, look for a good place to collect material to put in a terrarium. If you collected the litter in the deepest part of the woods, you may want to move to another area that receives more light. Light shade often supports an interesting assortment of living things: a rock with lichens growing on it, mushrooms, ferns, a small branch inhabited by ants, tree seedlings, and the like. Put them carefully into the large cardboard box. In the case of ferns, seedlings, grass, and other woodland plants, be sure to dig up the roots underneath along with their attached soil. It is best to leave animals such as snakes, toads, and salamanders in their native environment. When you get home, spray the plants with water from a mister.

8.

Examining Woodland Litter

In this activity, the child will examine the woodland litter brought back from the collecting trip to the woods. First, the immediately observable animal specimens (largely worms and insects) are removed and examined. The characteristics and properties of both the litter environment and the animals are studied. The number of animals of each kind in a given amount of litter is estimated and a classification scheme for the animals is devised. Thus this experience further develops skills and learning acquired in earlier activities.

After the larger animal specimens have been examined, a trapping device is set up to remove the tinier creatures from the litter. After they too are examined, the classification scheme is modified on the basis of the new findings.

MATERIALS

1 plastic bag of woodland litter
1 magnifying glass
1 popsicle stick, toothpick, or other litter probe
1 double sheet of newspaper
the child's measuring devices (the ruler and calibrated jar made in activities 5 and 6)
several small transparent jars with lids

1 large cardboard box that will hold a funnel and jar, as shown
  on page 50
1 compass
1 ruler, marked in both inches and centimeters
1 paring knife
1 pair of scissors
1 gooseneck lamp, or other movable light, with a 100-watt bulb
1 funnel, about 5 inches (13 cm) in diameter at the top
1 fine-screen, 14-inch mesh or wire gauze, large enough to
  cover the top of the funnel, as shown on page 50
1 sheet of black construction paper
plastic tape
1 round aluminum foil pan, about 4 inches (10 cm) in
  diameter
rubbing alcohol (optional)
microscope (optional)

PROCEDURE

A. Bring out the bag of woodland litter that you and the child
have collected. If the litter shows signs of drying out before
you are ready to use it, add as much as a cup of water to the
bag and let it sit for a day or two. In the meantime, you can
build the terrarium. It is very important for the litter to be
moist when the child examines it.

Spread out the sheets of newspaper on a table and put the
litter in a mound in the center. Ask the child to describe the litter. Since it is made up largely of organic detritus from different parts and different kinds of plants and trees, he will
probably see pieces of decaying leaves and whole leaves, rotting nuts, pieces of wood in the process of decomposition, ever-
green needles, and the like, depending on where the material
was collected. He may see a few animals but may not notice
animal remains. He should recognize the following properties

of the litter environment: It is moist, dark inside, and cool.

Next, carefully spread the litter out. Spread it into a layer no deeper than ¼ inch. Invite the child to take a close look at it. He can use a popsicle stick, toothpick, or other object to probe the litter. When he discovers an animal, the magnifying glass can be used to look at it up close. Avoid showing any signs of squeamishness in front of the child while examining the worms, insects, and other organisms that he discovers in the litter. Adopt a straightforward attitude that conveys the idea that you find the animals and their environment fascinating – which they are! Ask questions that invite comparisons, such as:

• How is this animal different from that one?

The child may or may not be able to identify earthworms, beetles, ants, centipedes, and spiders. It doesn't matter at this point. Focus on properties and look for similarities and dissimilarities among the animals. He should notice that some have legs and some don't. Of those with legs, some may have six and some eight. Some of the animals may have soft bodies and some hard outer coverings. Both qualitative and quantitative properties should be considered. The child will probably notice that some of the animals are bigger or longer than others. How much bigger or longer? Encourage him to measure their dimensions. He can use the ruler that he made, but the units may be too large for measuring the smaller animals. In that case, help him to measure them using the centimeter scale on the standard ruler. He can also fill his calibrated jar with litter and then count the number of animals he observes in that volume of material.

As the examination process continues, the child should begin to see some patterns. A classification scheme should begin to emerge. Putting animals with similar properties together will help to organize and emphasize the chosen classification. Bring out several small jars and help him to separate the animals into related groups. In some cases, there may be only one of a kind. For example, he might have a jar containing

only one large black ant and another jar with several small red ants. Keep the lids on the jars, but don't screw them tight.

After the most easily observable animals have been captured and put into the classification jars, ask the child if he noticed any animals that were too small to pick out of the litter. If he has been using a magnifying glass to make observations, he may have seen tiny wormlike and insectlike animals, so small that they were hard to pick up. It will be necessary to use a special kind of small trap to catch these tiny ones. Section B of this activity explains how to set up the trap.

Before putting away the litter, see if the child noticed any evidence that the animals have been causing changes in the litter material. Look for things like small pieces of bark that have holes in them. These were probably made by insects. It should be possible to see where leaves have been partially eaten by insects. He may have seen ants carrying bits of material. Explain that animals living in the litter help to create it: They slowly reduce the size of its particles and, in time, these become a part of the soil beneath the litter. The animals, which use the litter as food, also change in the process of growth and development. Their excrement, in turn, becomes part of the solid material within the litter environment. There is a complex interaction between the animals and their environment.

Return the litter to the plastic bag, sprinkle it well with water, tie the bag, and store it in a cool, dark place. As was indicated earlier, up to a cup of water can be added to make sure that the litter is soaked through before it is set aside. Remind the child that the litter was moist when you removed it from the bag. It will have dried out considerably during the time it was spread out on the newspapers. By adding water, you are attempting to return the litter environment to its original condition.

Now would be a good time to bring out some books on spiders, worms, and insects — after the child has worked out a classification system of his own. He may find, for instance, that some of the wormlike creatures in his classification are actually larval forms of certain insects. Thus he can be introduced to insect life cycles. There are many well-illustrated books for children on these subjects, including Herbert Zim's *Insects*.

B. Enlist the child's aid in setting up a trap for tiny insects:

1. Lay the large cardboard box on its side so that the open side faces you. In the center of the upper side, draw a circle 4 inches in diameter. This can be done with a compass. With a paring knife, cut the circle out of the box. You now have a hole which can be used to support the funnel.

2. Cut a 5-inch square out of the black construction paper and

lay it aside. Cover the outside of the funnel with the remainder of the black paper, so no light will enter from the side. Use the plastic tape to attach the paper to the funnel. Then insert the funnel into the hole you prepared in the box.
3. Put the fine screen on top of the funnel. Next, draw a circle 3 inches in diameter in the middle of the 5-inch square of black construction paper. Carefully cut out the circle without cutting through any sides of the square. Lay the construction paper, with the hole in the center, on top of the screen. Cut the bottom out of the aluminum foil pan and place it over the hole in the black paper. Place a small jar under the end of

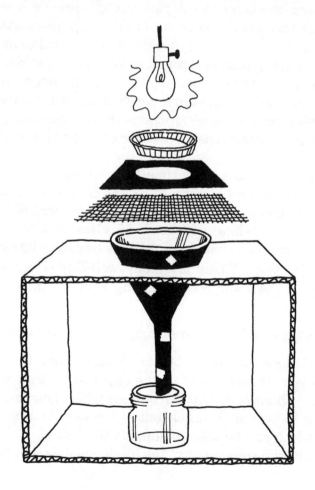

the funnel. Position the lamp so that its bulb is about 4 to 5 inches above the foil pan.

When a handful of woodland litter is placed in the bottomless pan on the screen, and the light turned on, the small insects will move downward, away from the light and heat. As they move away from the heat and light, they will fall through the screen into the funnel and then into the small jar. If you wish, about one inch of rubbing alchohol can be put into the jar. This will kill the insects and make it easier to examine them close up later on. Before beginning, however, review with the child the properties of the litter environment and prepare him for what you're going to do: Recall that it is moist, dark, and cool and then ask:
• What do you think the animals would do if the litter suddenly became hotter and brighter?

Encourage him to guess what might happen. Turn the lamp on and have him hold his hand underneath to feel the heat. Point out that the small animals are not used to the heat and light from the lamp. They will respond by moving downward, away from the heat and light. Then they will fall through the screen and into the jar.

At this point, if you have not already put a handful of litter into the aluminum foil pan over the screen, do so. (If you are using it, put some alcohol into the jar now and place it under the lower opening of the funnel.) Do it in this order because if the jar is put into place before the litter is put on the screen, small pieces of material are likely to fall into the jar. If the alcohol fumes bother you, you can fashion a collar for the jar out of aluminum foil, pressing it around the funnel opening. This will also slow evaporation of the alcohol. Orient the light so it is shining directly on the litter, and leave the setup for at least several hours. The child may want to check the jar occasionally during this time.

When a sufficient number of tiny animals have migrated out of the litter and been trapped in the jar, follow a procedure similar to that with the larger animals. Conduct a survey of the collection, looking for similarities and dissimilarities. The child will need to use the magnifying glass for this task. If a microscope is available, use it to look at the very tiniest animals. You may find tweezers useful in picking them up and putting them on a piece of paper or a slide. Help the child to realize that these animals have many properties in common with the larger ones and could be incorporated into the classification scheme. Discuss whether or not the scheme should be changed to include more categories. You might ask which jar this animal would go in, which jar that would go in, and the like, but don't try to actually put them in with the larger animals.

Before completing this activity, ask the child how the woodland litter should be disposed of. He might want to keep some of it to put into the terrarium. The best way of disposing of the remainder would be to return it to the same spot in the woods where the material was originally collected. This is not necessary, however. Find a spot outdoors under some trees or a bush where it is cool and shady and deposit the litter there. You won't be accused of littering!

9.

Building a Terrarium

A terrarium is a miniature land environment. It is an enclosed, self-contained system in which organisms characteristic of the larger environment from which they were taken are allowed to grow, reproduce, and interact with each other. Using the living material that he collected on the trip to the woods, the child will make a woodland terrarium that can be kept for some time as a reminder of his trip. The activity concludes with some suggestions for making additional self-contained systems which can enrich his understanding of the relationship between living things and their environment.

MATERIALS

the box of material collected during the walk in the woods
1 10-gallon glass aquarium tank with a glass cover (Sometimes an aquarium that leaks can be acquired inexpensively for use as a terrarium.)
crushed stone or gravel (This can come from a driveway or construction site.)
activated charcoal (available in pet stores)
1 spray mister containing water

PROCEDURE

First place the empty aquarium tank where you want the terrarium to be displayed. When the terrarium is filled, it will be
too heavy to move. Some factors to consider when deciding on
its location are light and temperature. See if the child realizes
this. The amount of light is particularly crucial. The terrarium
should not be in direct sunlight. Indirect or filtered sunlight
similar to that in the original setting is best. Remember that
you are trying to re-create that setting in miniature.

Put about 1½ to 2 inches of crushed stone or gravel into
the bottom of the tank to provide drainage. Mix some activated charcoal with the gravel and put some more on top. This
will prevent the overlying soil from turning sour. The child can
help you do this.

Check the box of woodland material that you collected.
Now you need to add soil to the terrarium. If there is not
enough in the box, supplement what there is with packaged
potting or terrarium soil. Don't use soil dug up outdoors,
because it will contain organisms foreign to the woodland environment. You will need enough soil to cover the roots of the
largest plants in the box. Here is where artistry begins to come
in. You and the child should shape the soil into the kind of
small hills and valleys that characterized the spot in the woods
where you did the collecting. For example, if you collected your
material from a hillside, make the soil slope like a hillside. Also,
keep in mind the direction from which the terrarium will be
viewed. If it will be seen from the front, with the back against
a wall, you might want to build up the soil with that in mind. If
you brought a good-sized rock back with you, put that in at
this time, somewhat off center or at the back. A fallen branch
or a piece of rotting wood can be positioned now, too. Arrange
the soil around it so the effect looks natural.

The final step is planting the plants. Start with the largest ones. These might be tree seedlings or ferns. Be sure their roots are well covered with soil. If the terrarium will be seen from the front, plant the largest plants in the back. Otherwise, they will obscure the rest. Plant the smaller plants in front and fill in with moss and woodland litter if that was found in the area. Don't plant too much or too close together. Remember that the plants will grow and spread out.

When the arrangement is completed, water the plants until a little water appears in the layer of gravel beneath the soil. Spray a fine mist of water on the ferns and moss. Then cover the terrarium to keep moisture in. Water will evaporate from the soil, condense on the underside of the cover, and drip back down on the plants, creating a water cycle within the system. (For sources of further information on terrariums, see the Book List, p. 107.)

Extensions

The terrarium you have made is composed principally of plant material. A child who is interested in insects might like to set up a self-contained system where he can study them. It is possible to set up an ant colony in a terrarium. Use a large glass jar. Dig into an ant colony and put worker ants, eggs, sand, and all into the jar. If you are lucky, you will find the ant

queen and can put her in too. This will ensure that the colony
grows. A small piece of damp sponge can provide water for the
ants. Put in a few rice grains or a sugar cube for a food supply.
Then cover the top of the jar with the screen you used for the
insect trap and wrap the jar in black construction paper or some
other opaque material. If you don't do this, the ants will make
all their tunnels inside the jar where you can't see them. After
three or four days, take the wrapping off and observe the
goings-on.

Another interesting project is to make a fruit-fly farm. As
the name implies, fruit flies are generally found around rotting
or fermenting fruit. These insects go through several stages in
their development from fertilized egg to adult. After the egg is
laid, it takes only a few days for it to hatch into a small wormlike creature called a larva. In several more days, the larva encases itself in a relatively hard little case and is called a
pupa. After a few days of development as a pupa, a full-grown
fruit fly emerges. The child may have observed such stages in
the insect life cycle in the woodland litter. In the case of fruit
flies, the entire process of development takes less than two
weeks, and he can observe generation after generation ap-
pearing.

Before starting the fruit-fly farm, you will need a see-
through plastic container. A good one for this purpose is the
container florists use for delivering corsages. These boxes
have a hinged lid that can easily be sealed with plastic tape.
An appropriate size is about 9 inches long, 6 inches wide, and 5
inches high. You will also need a food supply for the flies. A
good choice is an overripe banana, which can easily be obtained from a fruit market. There's a good chance that fruit
flies will have already laid eggs on the banana. You can check
by placing the banana in the container, closing it, and placing
it out of direct sunlight. Under such conditions, it is almost
certain that a first generation of adult flies will develop within
a few weeks. If none appear within two weeks, leave the container open for a few days. The distinctive odor of the ripened

banana will attract some flies. Once there is an established population, the lid of the container can be sealed with plastic tape. It will not be airtight. There will be a sufficient exchange of gases with the room to maintain the flies as long as the banana supplies them with food.

The child can use the magnifying glass to observe details within his fruit-fly farm. By holding the container in various positions relative to a light source, he should be able to see eggs, larvae, pupae, and adult flies. He should also note any changes in the interaction between the fruit flies and their environment: Does the banana get smaller in time? What happens to the number of flies?

IV
VARIABILITY IN PROPERTIES

10.

A Birthday Chart

If the child has done some of the preceding activities, she will be aware that it is possible to describe and classify objects according to their properties. She may also know that the value of a property can be assigned a number — that is, it can be measured. This and the following activities will develop the idea that even similar objects or events vary. Variability refers to the differences observed when you measure the same property of a group of seemingly identical objects or occurrences. For example, in activity 3, the child will have noticed that even in the *same* kind of seeds there were differences in germination times — all the radish seeds did not germinate simultaneously, for example.

This activity introduces the concept of variability by considering differences in the birthdays of family members. The child will record the months when they were born and then make a chart showing the distribution. This birthday chart is a bar graph representing the variability in birth months within the family.

MATERIALS

masking tape or rectangular gummed labels, ¾ inch (1.9 cm) wide

2 pieces of plain, unlined paper
1 pencil

PROCEDURE

Begin by making the framework for the birthday chart: Take a blank piece of unlined paper. With a ruler or other straight edge, draw a line parallel to the longer side of the paper but in from the edge far enough to allow for some writing. Draw another line perpendicular to this one (parallel to the shorter side of the paper) and in from its edge enough to allow for some writing there, too. Mark off twelve ¾-inch lengths along the longer line and write the abbreviated name of each month of the year, in order from left to right, below the line in each segment. Set this piece of paper aside for the time being.

Bring out the other piece of paper, which will serve as a record sheet. Ask the child what month she was born in and record it on the sheet next to her name. Write down the names of other family members below it and ask if she knows what months they were born in. Include aunts, uncles, grandparents, and cousins as well as members of the immediate family so that there are at least ten people on the list. She might want to include some of her friends too, especially if she has gone to a birthday party recently.

Next get out the ¾-inch masking tape or gummed labels. If you use tape, cut off several strips, each 1½ inches long. Cut off one strip for each person on your list. It is important that each strip have the same dimensions. Of course, if you use labels, they will already be the same dimensions. The ¾-inch width allows twelve pieces of tape or twelve labels to be lined up side by side along a piece of paper 11 inches long and still leaves room for some writing along the side of the chart. The 1½-inch length provides enough room to write a single name. (You may prefer to make your chart on a large piece of construction paper or stiff oak tag. In that case, correspond-

ingly larger strips of tape or gummed labels can be used.)
Write each name on the list on a different strip of tape or
gummed label. If you are using masking tape, it is somewhat
easier to write the names directly on the roll of tape, cut them
off one by one to the same length, and put them directly on the
chart.

Show the child the chart framework that you have set up.
• Aunt Nellie's birthday is in February. Where should we put
her tape?

Let her find February (or whatever month you have
named) on the month line at the bottom of the empty chart.
Then help her stick Aunt Nellie's tape or label down so that
one side is exactly on the line and the rest extends straight up
from there, making a bar on the chart graph. Try not to stick it
on crookedly.
• Here is your tape. Where should it go?
• Here is my tape. Where should mine go?

Eventually you will probably come to a person whose birth
month is the same as that of someone whose tape has already
been put on the graph. For instance, in the chart in the illustration, both Jan and Uncle Bob were born in October. Notice
that Jan's strip of tape is placed just above Uncle Bob's so that
the sides touch. You might want to draw a line where the edges
meet in such a case. Together, the two strips make a taller bar.
If there are three people with the same birth month, an even
taller bar will be formed. On the other hand, some months on
the chart may have no bars because no one in the family was
born in them.

After all the names have been properly attached to the
chart, the child will have a bar graph showing the variability of
birth months in the family. Such graphs are a useful way of
presenting information about variations. They show the range
or "scatter" of the data and tell how many individual members
of the group or population under study have a particular value
of the property in question.

1   2   3   4

JAN. | FEB. | MAR. | APR. | MAY | JUNE | JULY | AUG. | SEPT. | OCT. | NOV. | DEC.

| Grandma C. |
| Aunt N. |
| Cindy | Dad | Grandpa P. |
| Martha |
| Billy |
| Grandma P. |
| Connie |

| Mom |
| Uncle Bob | Jan |

| Me |

- In which month does our family have the greatest number of birthdays?

A question like this can help focus the child's attention on the fact that the height of the columns tells how many people had birthdays in that month. In the sample chart in the illustration, for example, the greatest number of birthdays occurred in March. This would be a good time to label the vertical axis on the chart. Write "Number of People" along the left side and fill in the numbers from 1 to 3 or 4, depending on your data, as shown in the illustration. The completed chart can then be displayed on a bulletin board or wall in the child's room.

11.

How Many Peas in a Pod?

Many phenomena in nature can best be described and understood in statistical terms. In this activity the child will again observe variability in the properties of a group — in this case, pea pods. In trying to answer the question how many peas there are in a pod, she will realize that she cannot answer it simply by opening up one pod and counting the number of peas it contains. The next pod that she opened would probably contain a different number. In order to answer such a question, it is necessary to open several pods and count the number of peas in each one. Of course, it is not possible to count all the peas in a large population of pods. Instead, the child will take a sample from such a population and count the number of peas in the sample pods. Based on her sample findings, she can then make inferences about the larger population.

During the course of the activity the child will make a tally of the number of peas in the sample pods. Then she will make a graph of the tally which will show the range in the number of peas in a pod and the most frequent value. Such a graph is called a histogram. Like the birthday chart in activity 10, this graph is a useful way of summarizing information about variations.

MATERIALS

1 brown paper or other opaque bag to hold 30 pea pods
30 fresh green pea pods, plus a few extra
2 pieces of lined paper
2 copies of the graph paper grid on page 69 (The graph paper
    will also be used in the next activity, so you might want to
    make several copies at once.)
1 felt-tip marking pen or colored pencil

PROCEDURE

A. Show the child one of the pea pods and ask her how many
peas she thinks are in it. Let her open it and count the peas inside. Be sure she counts only the developed peas and not the
undeveloped nodes which are sometimes present. Explain that
the peas are seeds, and that some develop and some don't.

Take out a second pod and ask:
• How many peas do you think you'll find in this pod?

She may or may not think the number will be the same as
in the first pod. If it is the same, have her open a third pod and
count the peas. Establish the idea that the number of peas in a
pod varies. It is likely that she will get a different number each
time. To find out how many peas there are in a pod, it will be
necessary to open several pods, count the number of peas in
each, and find out what the range of values is. It would be
great if your child could count all the peas in a large population
of pods – for example, all those in a given store. She would get
a very accurate set of values for the number of peas in a pod.
But since it's usually not possible to study that many pods,
she can take a representative *sample* from the population,
study the property in question in the sample, and then use
that information to make inferences about the larger population.

Take out the bag containing the 30 pea pods. The bag should be made of brown paper or some other opaque material. For the time being, the contents of the bag can be considered the population of pea pods. The child will take a sample of pods from the bag, one at a time, count the number of peas in each pod, and record it. In order to ensure that she gets an unbiased representative sample, she must pick the pods at random. Tell her you are going to play a game similar to a party grab-bag game. Then ask her to shut her eyes, reach into the bag of pods, and take one out without looking into the bag. She should then open the pod and count the number of peas it contains. This number should be recorded next to the number 1 (for the first pod) on a sheet of lined paper. Number down the paper from 1 to 10 for the total sample of 10 pods. Next, the child should select a second pod, count the number of peas in it, and record that number. She should keep going until she has counted the number of peas in all 10 pods and recorded

each number. The number of peas in a pod is likely to vary between 2 and 8, although it may be as low as 0 and as high as 9.

Now show the child the graph paper grid and suggest that she try making a graph of the number of peas she found in the sample pods. Help her get started by labeling the axes of the graph for her: The vertical axis should be labeled "Number of Peas"; the horizontal axis should be labeled "Pods." Leave room along the vertical axis to fill in the numbers representing the number of peas. Leave room along the horizontal axis to fill in the number of each pod, as shown in Figure 1. Notice that the numbers are placed in the middle of each space.

Above the number 1 on the horizontal axis, which is the column where the number of peas counted in the first pod will be represented, the child should use the felt-tip pen or colored pencil to color in the same number of squares as there were peas in that pod. One square stands for one pea. In Figure 1, which shows what one child found, three squares are colored in the first column because the first pod selected from the bag contained three peas. Once your child has filled in the first column, she can go on to show the number of peas she counted in the second pod in the second column, labeled 2. Having had the initial experience with graphing in activity 10, she should get the idea fairly rapidly. Have her continue until the data on all 10 pods are shown on the graph. If there is a pod with no peas in it, no squares would be colored in above that number.

Before concluding this section of the activity, return to the original question:

• How many peas are in a pod?

It should be clear by now that there is no single answer to the question. The data show a range of values. One answer would be to give the range, or spread, of values. In Figure 1, the lowest number of peas was 2 and the highest number was 6. Thus the range is 4 peas – the difference between the highest and lowest values. This is one measure of variability.

If you had to give a single answer to this question, it might be the most frequent value – that is, the number of peas

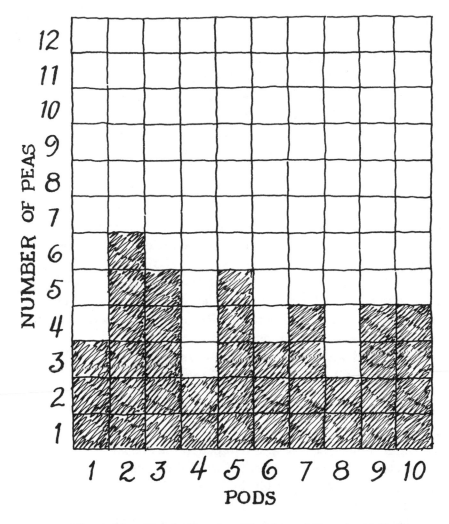

Fig. 1. Bar Graph Showing Number of Peas in 10 Pods

that was found most often. In Figure 2, the most frequent value was 4. Three pods out of ten had 4 peas in them. Because of the way the graph is set up, however, the most frequent value is not immediately apparent, nor is the range. In the next section of this activity, the child will make a tally of her findings on a larger sample of pea pods and make what is called a histogram of the data that will show the range and most frequent value at a glance.

B. In section A, the child found that the number of peas in a pod ranged between two values. Suppose she counted the number of peas in a larger sample. Would she get the same range and most frequent value? There were 30 pods in the bag to start with. She took out a sample of 10, so there should be 20 pods left in the bag. If she were to count the number of peas in those pods, she would have a larger sample of 30 pods altogether. These 30 pods could be regarded as a sample of all the pods in the store where they were bought. In other words, they can be considered a sample of a larger population. Usually, the larger the sample you use, the more reliable the inferences drawn.

Have the child count the number of peas in the remaining 20 pods and add the count to the list of 10 she started on the lined paper. She should end up with a list of 30 pods and the number of peas found in each.

• How could we represent all these values on the graph?

There is no way of adding these 20 pods to the child's existing graph, because it is only 10 squares wide. She would need graph paper 30 squares wide to show the number of peas in 30 pods as it is set up now. Of course, she could paste or tape two additional sheets of graph paper to the one she already has completed. But there is another way of representing the data that will allow her to get all the information on one new sheet of graph paper.

Take out a second sheet of lined paper. Ask the child to look at the list of 30 pods on the first sheet and find the *lowest* number of peas. Write this number down on the second sheet of paper. Then ask her to look on the list for the *highest* number of peas that she found in the 30 pods. (These numbers may or may not be the same numbers she found for the limits of the range in the 10-pod sample.) Down the left side of the second sheet of paper, write the range of values, from the lowest number to the highest. In the tally sheet in Figure 2, the number ranged from 2 peas per pod to 8 peas per pod. Now make another column to the right of the one labeled "Number of Peas in Each Pod." Label this second column "Number of Pods." Then have the child go down the list of 30 pods on the first sheet of paper, one at a time, and make a mark for each pod under the "Number of Pods." For example, suppose the first pod on her list contained 3 peas. She would make a mark for that pod to the right of the 3. If the second pod had 6 peas in it, she would make a mark for that pod to the right of the 6, and so on. When she has gone through the entire list of 30 pods, she will end up with a tally something like the one in Figure 2.

Number of Peas in Each Pod	Number of Pods
2	TTTT
3	TTTT I
4	TTTT IIII
5	TTTT II
6	II
7	
8	I

Fig. 2. Tally Sheet

In making tallies, most people make a slash for every fifth mark, but this is not necessary. However, there should be 30 marks, one for each pod. If there aren't, go back over the list until you find the error.

Now take out a second sheet of graph paper. The child may have noticed that the tally looks like a bar graph already, especially if it is turned so that the numbers are at the bottom. Using the tally, she should make a graph with the number of peas in each pod represented along the horizontal axis and the number of pods along the vertical axis. The axes should be labeled accordingly. Notice that in this graph, or histogram, the numbers along the axes stand for something different from what they did in the first graph. In that graph of the 10-pod sample, the numbers along the vertical axis stood for the number of *peas,* and each colored-in square stood for 1 pea. Here, each colored-in square stands for 1 *pod.* Thus there should be 30 squares colored in, just as there were 30 marks on the tally. A histogram based on the tally above is shown in Figure 3.

Unlike the bar graph made earlier, the histogram shows the range of values and the most frequent value at a glance. In the 30-pod sample, a pod with 8 peas turned up. Thus the range is broader here than in the smaller sample — from 2 to 8 peas, or 6 peas. The most frequent value is simply the highest column on the histogram. In this case, the value that came up most often was 4 peas: 9 of the pods had 4 peas in them. The most frequent value is called the mode of the distribution. Here the mode of the 30-pod sample is the same as the mode of the 10-pod sample. This is not always the case. Your child may find different values for the mode in her larger and smaller samples of pods.

• Suppose you opened up another pea pod. How many peas do you think you would find inside?

The most important idea to get across here is that the property of a single item cannot be predicted with certainty. The best prediction would be that the number of peas in the

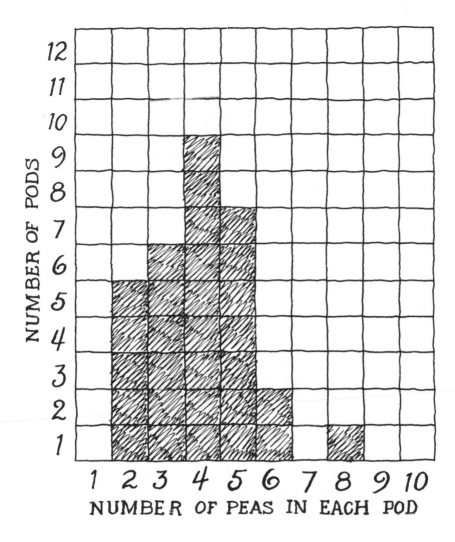

Fig. 3. Histogram Showing Number of Peas in 30 Pods

next pod would fall somewhere in the range of values in the larger sample. If the child wants to make a single "best guess" as to what she will find in the next pod, she can choose the most frequent value in the larger sample. But there is no assurance that this guess will be verified on opening the pod!

12.

How Many Children in a Family?

Families can be described in many different ways: according to the national origin of the parents, the number of living grandparents, the age of family members, and so on. Another property of families that varies is the number of children in them. In this activity the child will list the number of children in several families, including her own. She will then represent the data both graphically and with a set of building blocks. By "evening off" the blocks, she will find the average number of children in this sample group of families. After getting a feel for what an average is by repositioning the blocks, she will use a similar procedure to find the mean, or average, number of children on the graph.

MATERIALS

1 copy of the graph paper on page 69
1 set of child's building blocks
1 piece of paper, lined or unlined
2 felt-tip marking pens or colored pencils, each a different color
1 pencil

PROCEDURE

A. Begin by asking the child how many children there are in her family. Start a list by writing down the number next to her name on the piece of paper. Go on from there to other families that she is acquainted with: those of her friends, cousins, and the like. Next to each family name, have her write down the number of children in that family. Keep going until you have 10 families in all. Families that have no children can also be included.

Bring out the copy of the graph paper grid and ask the child to get out her building blocks. There should be as many blocks as there are children on the list.

• How could we show the number of children in your family on the graph?

Suppose there are 2 children in the family. Then the number of children could be represented by a column 2 squares high on the graph. With the building blocks, one block would be placed directly on top of another. (One square or one block stands for one child.) With a colored pen or pencil, have the child color in the bottom 2 squares in the first column on the left on the graph paper. This column represents the first family (her own) in the sample. She can label it with her initials or with the number 1.

Now go on to the second family on the list. Suppose there is one child in that family. That child would be represented by one square or by one building block. Using the same color as before, have the child color in the bottom square in the second column from the left on the graph paper. At the same time, she should put one of her building blocks right next to the pile of 2 that she has set up to represent her own family. Don't leave any space between piles. The only time there should be a space (or an uncolored square at the bottom of the graph) is when there are no children in one of the families.

Continue with this procedure with each of the remaining families on the list. There are 10 columns on the graph paper grid, one for each family. This bar graph is similar to the one made to represent the number of peas in the sample of 10 pods. Each column should be colored in with the same number of squares as there are children in that particular family. Similarly, the child should end up with a row of blocks in which the height of each column is equivalent to the number of children in that family. In the case of the blocks, it often helps if the columns are lined up against a wall; the child can keep the columns in a row more easily that way. When she is finished, she should have a graph and a row of blocks that look the same. The only difference is that the graph is two-dimensional and the block setup is a three-dimensional representation of variations in the number of children in families.

B. With the graph and building block setup in front of her, ask the child how many children there are in a family. See if she realizes there is no single answer to this question. The number of children in a family varies, just as the number of peas in a pod varies.

• What is the range in the number of children in the families?

In this sample of 10 families, the lowest number of children might have been 0 and the highest number 6. In that case the range would be 6. This number describes the spread in values. Of course, in another sample of 10 families, the spread in values might be different.

Another number which is useful in describing a population is the mean, or average, value. The child can find the mean number of children in the families in her sample using the block representation. Tell her that if she evens off the blocks, she will be able to find the average number of children in a family. One at a time, have her move the blocks from higher positions to lower positions, until no more lowering can be done. For instance, she might start by taking the block at the very top of a column standing for the family with 6 children and put it on one of the blocks that stands for a family with one child. She should keep shifting the blocks until all the lower spaces have been filled in and the peaks and troughs have been evened off. The block setup will then look generally flat on top but will probably have a few extra blocks sticking up here and there.

• What is the average number of children in the families?

Look at the height of the blocks now. Suppose the general height is 2 blocks high, with a few columns having 3 blocks. Then the average number of children in the sample of 10 families is more than 2. It is greater than 2 and less than 3.

Now have the child carry out the evening-off procedure on the bar graph she has made. Give her a contrasting-colored pen or pencil and have her cross out one of the higher squares with an X and color in one of the lower squares. This is equivalent to repositioning the blocks from higher to lower positions. She should keep crossing out higher squares and filling in lower squares until the graph is evened off as much as pos-

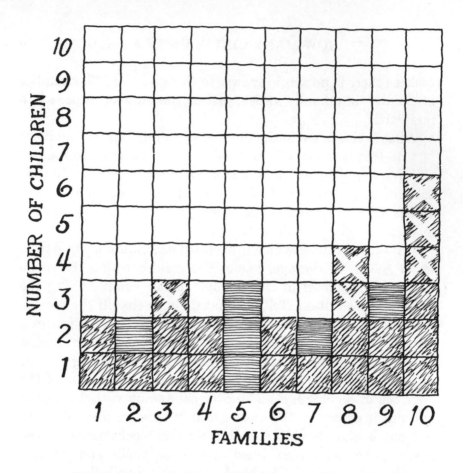

Fig. 1. Graph Showing the Mean Number of Children in
a Group of Families

sible. As with the blocks, there will come a point at which it is
possible to shift further but no more lowering can be effected.
At that point, she will have found the average value. It should
be exactly the same as the one she found by evening off the
blocks. In Figure 1, the evened-off value is 2, with 3 squares
left above the general level. Thus the best single figure to express the mean number of children in a family, based on this
limited sample, is 2. If the evening-off procedure had resulted
in every column having 3 squares filled in, except one which
had only 2, the average would still be greater than 2 and less
than 3. But in that case, the best single figure to express the

mean would be 3, because it would be closer to that value. Whatever the final value, however, this activity should help the child acquire an intuitive understanding of what an average is and how it may be used to describe a population with variable properties.

Extension

If you feel the child can handle it, you can introduce her to an interesting technique for finding the average (mean) number of children in the sample families using a histogram. First make a tally showing the number of children in each family. In the sample tally in Figure 2, the data are the same as those obtained in parts A and B of this activity.

Fig. 2. Tally Sheet

Number of Children in Each Family	Number of Families
0	|
1	||
2	||||
3	|
4	|
5	
6	|

Now make a histogram of the data using the building blocks. You can label the blocks by putting the numbers representing the number of children in each family on slips of paper in front of each column of blocks.

Once the three-dimensional histogram is set up, the child can find the average by "piling in" the blocks from either end. Begin by shifting a block with the lowest value *up* one space *in value*. Then she can shift a block with the highest value *down* one space *in value*. The blocks may or may not shift up or down in the vertical dimension in the process. It should be a balanced operation, with a block moving in toward the center from the right, then another moving in toward the center from the left, then one from the right, and so on, one space at a time. What you are doing is piling in the blocks toward the average, mean value. The left side of Figure 3 shows the start of this process in a building-block histogram representing the data in the tally in Figure 2. The right side of Figure 3 shows the blocks at the end of the process, piled up around the average.

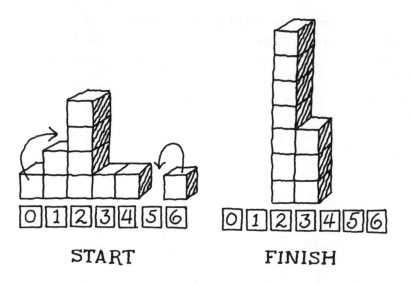

START   FINISH

Fig. 3. Finding the Mean on a Three-Dimensional Histogram

The average should be the same as the one you got earlier by crossing out squares on the two-dimensional graph. It is possible to make a histogram from the tally on a sheet of the graph paper, as you did in activity 11, and then "pile in" the squares on the graph to find the mean, but the crossings-out tend to become confusing. The process is clearer using the blocks.

V
PATTERNS AND RELATIONSHIPS

13.

Taste: Mapping the Tongue

This and the following activities focus on the patterns and relationships within properties. Many patterns exist in nature that are not immediately visible – for example, the patterns of tasting. The surface of the tongue shows bumps and ridges, all of which look alike. In fact, however, the tongue is differentiated into areas specialized for different kinds of tastes – salt, sweet, sour, and bitter. In this activity, the child discovers how these areas are arranged on the tongue, and then "maps" the hidden pattern.

MATERIALS

water
small amounts of salt, sugar, lemon juice, and vanilla extract
1 1-ounce (approximately 30 ml) plastic or wax paper cup, or
   other small container
Cotton swabs
2 or more copies of the tongue outline on page 89
4 different-colored pencils or crayons

PROCEDURE

A. Ask the child to look at his tongue up close in a mirror. Let him look at your tongue too, with a magnifying glass if he wishes.

• What do you see on the tongue?

He will see small bumps and ridges, all of which look about the same, both on his tongue and on yours. (The so-called "taste buds" are in the hollows, but these cannot be seen even with a magnifying glass.)

Now suggest that he try testing his tongue to see how and where different foods are tasted. Of course, most foods are made up of different ingredients with a combination of flavors. He will be testing his tongue with four different solutions, each of which has a single flavor or taste. The problem will be to find out where the tongue tastes each one.

Start with a sugar solution. Take the 1-ounce cup or other small container and fill it about half full of water. Put in a small amount of sugar — ¼ teaspoon will be plenty. Stir it until the sugar dissolves. Then the child can dip a cotton swab in the solution and carefully swab his tongue all over. After doing so, he should close his mouth, wait a minute, and try to locate the places where he gets the strongest sensation of sweet taste. It is important to wait a minute before trying to locate the places on the tongue that react to particular tastes because it is the residual sensation you are trying to detect, not the immediate one that may be experienced all over the tongue. After the child has done this, try it yourself and see if you agree on where the strongest sensation of sweetness is located. Here is a hint: Ask him how an ice-cream cone tastes and how he licks it!

After he has made up his mind about where the sweetness is tasted on his tongue, the child can color in the corresponding

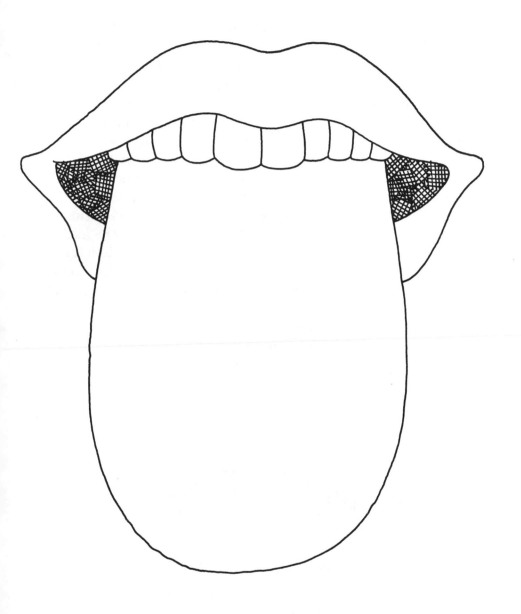

area on the copy of the tongue above. He might want to turn the drawing of the tongue upside down so it faces in the same direction as his tongue when it is stuck out.

When you have finished testing the sweet solution, discard it along with used swabs. Rinse out your mouths with water. Then rinse out the small cup thoroughly and make the sour solution. Again fill the small cup half full of water, but this time add a little strained lemon juice to the water. A few drops of the juice will probably be enough in ½ ounce of water. Using the sour solution soon after the sweet one increases the sensitivity to the sour taste, but you don't want the solution to be so puckery that the child will find it repellent. The idea is just to find out where the sour tastes are tasted. Let him try to find out using a second swab. Again he should swab his tongue all over, wait a minute, and try to detect where he is tasting sourness the most. If he's not sure, he can rinse out his mouth with water and try it again.

With a different color, the child should color in the area on the tongue outline that best corresponds to the area(s) where the sour taste of the lemon juice solution was the strongest. He can put a key at the bottom of the paper to indicate which

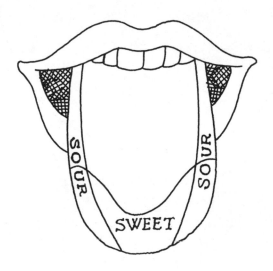

color stands for which taste, or he can write the tastes on the map. An idealized diagram, showing where sweet and sour tastes are actually detected, is shown here for your reference. Don't expect your child to come up with a map that clearly differentiated. Accept his conclusions as they are.

B. After tasting the sweet and sour substances, take a break. When you come back, give the child a fresh copy of the tongue outline to record where the salty and bitter substances are tasted. It will be less confusing than trying to put all four areas on one outline.

The salt solution is made in the same way that the sweet solution was made. Start with the 1-ounce cup about half full of water. Put a pinch of salt into the water and stir until it dissolves. Then the child can swab his tongue with the salty solution, wait a minute as before, and try to decide where the strongest sensation of saltiness is located on his tongue. He should record this on the second tongue outline.

Finally, have him try the vanilla extract solution. Be sure to thoroughly rinse out the salt solution from the small container before refilling it half full of water. Add one or two drops of extract. With a fresh swab, he can then spread this solution on his tongue. The bitter taste is harder to localize than the others. Also, vanilla extract is slightly aromatic, so the child may be confused by a sweet smell along with the bitter taste. See if he gets the same location for the bitter taste when he holds his nose.

As shown in the diagram, bitter substances are tasted at the back of the tongue. (You may have noticed this when you take aspirin, which is very bitter. If a tablet is placed at the back of the tongue, in hopes it will go down more quickly, the bitter taste becomes apparent the minute it starts to dissolve. If it is placed on the front of the tongue, there is no bitter taste at all, no matter how long it's left there.) Again, a diagram is included for your reference only and should not be imposed on the child as "the right answer."

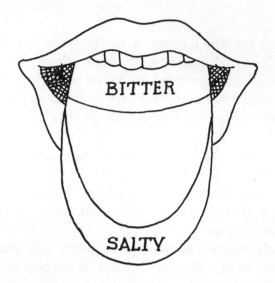

• Where on your tongue are sweet, sour, salty, and bitter things tasted?

Once a hidden pattern of taste is revealed by the test results, encourage the child to describe the pattern in words. Besides developing verbal facility, this will help consolidate the experience in his mind.

14.

Sound: The Fishline Harp

In this activity, the child will gradually begin to notice the relationship between the length of a tube, string, or bar on a musical instrument and how low or high the sound is – that is, its pitch. He will make his own stringed instrument, a small harp, and with it will recognize that sound is produced by moving or vibrating parts. The longer the vibrating string on the harp, the lower the pitch; the shorter the string, the higher the pitch. By examining and listening to other instruments as well, he will begin to predict which part will produce a higher or lower note.

MATERIALS

1 box of drinking straws
1 pair of child's scissors
1 10-foot (3 m) length of 6-pound nylon fishline, obtainable at sporting goods and hardware stores
1 piece of corrogated cardboard, approximately 9 by 7 inches (18 by 23 cm)
1 pair of shears
1 pencil

plastic tape
an assortment of musical instruments, such as a xylophone, a
   harmonica, a "Pan's pipe," a guitar, etc. These may be toys.

PROCEDURE

A. Take a drinking straw from the box and ask the child if he
can make a sound with it. After he has had a chance to try,
take another straw and try it yourself. To do this, hold the
straw upright and blow across the top. You should be able to
produce a reasonably clear note. Let the child practice until he
can do it too. Then take his scissors and, after you have
sounded the note again, cut off about an inch from the bottom
of the straw. Blow across the top again.
• What do you hear?
   The sound will be perceptibly higher. Let him tell you this
in his own words. Then try it again, cutting off another inch
from the bottom of the straw.
• What do you hear this time?
   The note you blow will be higher still. By now, the child
will probably want to try this himself, so give him a fresh
straw and the scissors and listen while he makes progressively
higher notes for you. Several segments of straw can be cut off,
leaving a very short straw that will produce a relatively high-
pitched note. This is so much fun and so simple to do that the
two of you may run through the whole box of straws! Without
pressing for any single "correct" formulation, encourage the
child to express what he thinks the relationship is while he
plays around with them. See if he can play a short tune with
the different lengths of straws.
B. What you made with the straws was a very simple wind instrument. Of course, it's not very easy to play a tune on it,
because the different lengths of straws have to be picked up
and blown one after the other. Suggest to the child that he
make a stringed instrument that can be played more easily.

Show him the materials you have assembled to make the harp and ask if he knows of any musical instruments with strings. Most young children will mention guitars and violins even if such instruments are not played in the home. If you have a piano and can open it to show the strings, do so. Most children don't realize that the piano is a stringed instrument and that it has a sounding board inside that looks like a harp. While you are chatting, help him to make the fishline harp:

1. He should begin by covering opposite ends of the piece of cardboard with strips of plastic tape. This will reinforce the edges where the fishline will be wound.
2. Using the shears, cut pairs of slits in two diagonally opposite corners of the cardboard. Notching the cardboard takes some strength, so do this yourself.
3. Working together, wind one end of the fishline about ten times through the slits in one corner of the cardboard. Then pull on the line with a steady force while stringing about six

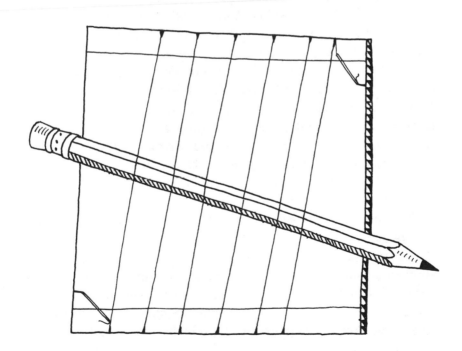

equally spaced, lengthwise turns around the cardboard. Then wind the fishline about ten times through the other pair of slits. The hardest part is getting the line started on the cardboard. Taping the starting end down sometimes helps. Additional tape may be used to secure the ends.

4. Insert a pencil at a slight angle across the cardboard under the strings.

After he has had a chance to play with the harp freely, ask the child questions like these:

• What part of the harp moves while the sound is made? How do you know?

Children will usually say that it is the string that makes the sound, and they know because they can see it move while they hear the sound. You can say that the string vibrates.

• Which strings make the highest sounds? Which ones make the lowest sounds? What can you do to the harp to change the pitch?

In most cases, the shortest string will produce the highest pitch and the longest string the lowest. The pencil bridge divides each string into two parts. Unless the bridge is in the middle of the card, one part will have a higher pitch and the other a lower pitch. This is because one part of each string will differ from the other in length. The child should make this discovery for himself by setting the pencil at different angles. The pitch is also affected by the thickness of the string and how tight it is. Thus he may find some strings "out of order" in pitch if they are tighter or looser than the rest. In general, however, the shorter strings produce the higher sounds and the longer strings lower sounds.

• How are the sounds made by the harp like the sounds made by the straws?

At this point, the child should begin to see the pattern: the longer the part, the lower the sound; the shorter the part, the higher the sound. The shorter lengths of straws produced the higher notes and so did the shorter lengths of string on the harp. The longer lengths produced the lower notes. Often young children will grasp the relationship intuitively without being able to verbalize it. They need to be encouraged to express it in words.

C. If the child has a toy xylophone, bring it out now. If he doesn't have one, this would be a good time to get one. If you have either a toy or a real harmonica, try to remove the back cover so that he can see the reeds of different lengths inside. So-called Pan's pipes are not as common, but if you have one, the child should be able to see the connection between this instrument and the activity with the straws of different lengths. He can even make a Pan's pipe by simply gluing straws of increasing lengths side by side onto a backing. As in a xylophone, the segments should increase in length by equal amounts.

• What parts of the xylophone do you think will make the high notes?

• What parts do you think will make the low notes? Encourage him to predict what he will hear *before* he plays the instrument. See if he says that the shorter bars on the xylophone will produce the higher notes and the longer bars the lower notes. This will tell you whether or not he has gotten the idea. Then let him check his prediction by trying it.

Extensions

These activities can be enriched in a variety of ways: for instance, if there is a church nearby that has an organ with visible pipes, take the child to see it. Which pipes does he think will make the low notes? Which pipes will make the high notes? Some churches in large cities have a series of bells of increasing size, called a carillon, that can be visited. And, of course, this would be a good time to take the child to a children's concert of instrumental music.

Children often enjoy composing short, distinctive sequences of notes on their instruments to represent themselves, their dolls, or their animals. These sound patterns or melodies are like codes. You can motivate them to try this by playing sections of a recording of Prokofiev's *Peter and the Wolf* or Ravel's *Mother Goose Suite*. These compositions contain sections in which particular instruments play both alone and together to represent various animals and people.

15.

Color: Chromatography with Paper Towels

One of the most fascinating and pleasing properties of an object is its color. In this final activity, the child will return to the property of color, first encountered in activity 1. He will find that just as there are hidden patterns of taste, color also reveals unexpected patterns. He will test an assortment of colored inks on paper towels and discover that, although each appears to be one homogeneous color, some of the inks are actually mixtures of different-colored substances. When drops of water fall on the ink spots, the colors separate into their component parts, forming radial patterns on the towels. This is because the different-colored components travel through the paper at different rates. Just as a faster runner will gradually outdistance a slower one, even though both left the starting point together, colored material that can move through the paper more rapidly will gradually separate from material that moves more slowly.

MATERIALS

1 roll of plain white paper towels
1 set of felt-tip marking pens, containing water-soluble, non-permanent ink, in assorted colors
assorted food colorings (optional)
1 eye dropper
1 small container of water

PROCEDURE

Tear off several sheets of paper towel. Show the child how to fold each of the sheets in half and then in half again to make four layers. The folded rectangles of toweling will be about 30 square inches in area.

Next, take one of the rectangles of toweling and show the child how to make a small circle ¼ to ½ inch in diameter in the center of the top layer with one of the felt-tip marking pens. Gently color in the circle so as not to tear the towel. In one corner of the rectangle, make a dot or other mark with the pen to identify the color of the ink later. Alternatively, you could write the name of the color on the edge of the paper.

After he has seen what to do, have the child help prepare the rest of the towels. Each piece should have a different-colored circle of ink in the center of it and an identifying mark at the edge in the same color. You might want to try food coloring on a few pieces of toweling for comparison. Green food coloring is usually particularly interesting. If the food coloring bottles do not have openings that release only a small drop of color, use a cotton swab to make the small circle of color on the towel.

When the towels are ready, the child should get some water in a small container. An eye dropper or medicine dropper

will be used to put drops of water on the colored circle on each piece of toweling, one at a time. Tell him to put about 10 drops of water directly on the center of each inked circle. Count the 10 drops carefully so that he won't drench the towel with too much water.

• What happens when the water is dropped on the colored circles?

As you watch, the ink will spread out from the center with the water. A pattern of ragged, circular bands of color will form wherever the ink is composed of more than one colored component. Some inks, such as black and brown, yield especially interesting patterns. Ask the child how many colored parts these inks seem to have and which color is farthest from the center.

• Why are some colors farther from the center than others?

The colors that are farther from the center moved more rapidly with the water through the paper. These components go a greater distance in the same amount of time than the slower components. This is why the colors separate and a pattern emerges.

• What would you expect to see if the ink were made of only one color?

If the ink were composed of only one color component, the color would spread out from the center, forming a larger ragged circle, but no different-colored bands would form. In fact, this is what happens with some inks. For example, both red and yellow inks and food colorings often do not separate because they are made of only one color. They look uniform and homogeneous, and they are. No hidden pattern will emerge in these cases. The child may be disappointed in them, but try to emphasize the conclusions that can be drawn from such observations: Either the inks must be composed of only one kind of substance or, if they are composed of more than one, the others are not soluble in water. The latter explanation is unlikely with pens that are sold as containing washable, nonpermanent inks.

• Do any of the same colors show up in more than one of the inks?

Many of the colored components are repeated in the inks, but in different combinations and proportions. Encourage the child to compare his results in order to establish this idea. Comparison will also establish that the order of separation is not haphazard. The pattern for a particular ink is fixed, given the same medium (paper) and the same solvent (water). Thus the pattern can be used to identify the ink, just as a fingerprint can identify a person. In the extensions to this activity, the child can experiment with a different kind of paper and with chalk to see how these media affect the hidden patterns of the inks.

Extensions

With coffee filter paper, you can approximate the actual technique of liquid chromatography, in which the liquid travels up a medium, carrying other substances with it. In this case, the different-colored components of the inks or food colorings will separate out as water travels up the filter paper.

Get out a tall, clear drinking glass. Don't use one that is made of colored glass or has designs on it. With scissors, cut a strip from the filter paper that is slightly longer than the height of the glass. Next, unbend and straighten out a paper clip so it can be threaded through one end of the paper strip as shown in the figure. The clip will be used to hang the strip of paper in the glass. Test it to be sure the paper does not touch the bottom of the glass. If it does, cut off a bit of paper from the bottom of the strip.

Now you are ready to put the circle of ink or food color on the paper. As you did with the paper towels, color in a circle ¼ to ½ inch in diameter. The dab of color should be placed about 2 inches above the bottom end of the paper. This is so it will be above the water level when a small amount of water is put into the glass. Use some of the colors that you know from the paper towel activity contain at least two components. That way you can compare the order of separation you get in the different papers. You can set up as many strips as you want in different glasses.

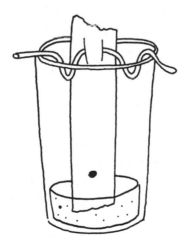

When the strips of filter paper are all prepared, put small amounts of water in the bottoms of the glasses. Then put the strips in. The water should not directly touch the colored dab on the paper, nor should the strip cling to the walls of the glass. Within a few seconds, the water will travel up the paper and reach the colored spot. As it continues to travel upward, the colored material will begin to separate into its different components. Again, the separation takes place because the different parts travel up the paper at different rates. In one sample of green food color, for instance, a blue component traveled ahead, leaving a yellowish-green color behind. If the paper is left in the water long enough, the slower-moving colors will "catch up" and the different components will recombine to form the original color again. However, the child may want to take the strip out before this happens so he will have a record of the separation. If so, he can remove the strip from the glass when the colored material has moved about three-quarters of the way up the paper and let the strip dry.

It is also interesting to compare the color separation results obtained in an entirely different medium. This can be done using one or more pieces of unused, soft (dusty), white chalk. In this case, use the pen to draw a narrow band of color around the piece of chalk near the bottom. A cotton swab or toothpick can be used to do this with food coloring. Each piece of chalk should be encircled completely. Then the piece of chalk should be stood upright in a small container of water, such as a 1-ounce cup. The colored band should be above the water level in the cup. Within a minute or two, the band of color will start to get wider as the water moves up the chalk. After ten or fifteen minutes, the child can remove the chalk, pour the water out of the cup, and replace the chalk in position in the empty cup. Since there will be a great deal of water inside the chalk, the color separation process will continue.

When you compare the records of separation in filter paper

with the separation of the same material in chalk, you may be surprised. One child found that whereas the blue component in green food coloring traveled ahead of the yellow in paper, in chalk the yellow traveled ahead of the blue. Try it and see!

Book List

This is a list of some of the books available for adults and young children that deal with the subjects of the science activities you have just read about. There are many books about some of the subjects, such as nature study; there are too few books about others, such as elementary statistics. The list reflects what is available.

Behrens, June. *The True Book of Metric Measurement.* Chicago: Children's Press, 1975. For the youngest readers.

Buck, Margaret Waring. *In Woods and Fields.* New York: Abington, 1950. Excellent but out of print. May be available in libraries.

Busch, Phyllis S. *Wildflowers and the Stories Behind Their Names.* New York: Scribner, 1977. Beautifully illustrated.

Conklin, Gladys. *Fairy Rings and Other Mushrooms.* New York: Holiday House, 1973.

Davis, Bette J. *Winter Buds.* New York: Lee & Shepard, 1973.

Dowden, Anne Ophelia. *Wild Green Things in the City: A Book of Weeds.* New York: Crowell, 1972. Beautifully illustrated.

Eberle, Irmengarde. *Fawn in the Woods.* New York: Crowell, 1962. A story with photographs by Lilo Hess.

Fey, James T. *Long, Short, High, Low, Thin, Wide.* New York: Crowell, 1971. One of a series edited by Dr. Max Beberman, Director of the Committee on School Mathematics Projects at the University of Illinois. *Graph Games* by Frédérique and Papy is another book in this series, in which the reading level is appropriate for young children.

Gallob, Edward. *City Leaves, City Trees.* New York: Scribner, 1972. Highly recommended – a winner of the Children's Science Book Award of the New York Academy of Sciences.

Gallob, Edward. *City Rocks City Blocks and the Moon.* New York: Scribner, 1973.

Hess, Lilo. *Small Habitats.* New York: Scribner, 1976.

Hopf, Alice L. *Biography of an Ant.* New York: Putnam, 1974.

Hutchins, Ross E. *The Amazing Seeds.* New York: Dodd Mead, 1960.

Lavine, Sigmund A. *Wonders of Terrariums.* New York: Dodd Mead, 1977.

Leaf, Munro. *Metric Can Be Fun.* Philadelphia: Lipincott, 1976. A paperback for children in grades 1 to 3.

List, Albert Jr., and Ilka K. List. *A Walk in the Forest: The Woodlands of North America.* New York: Crowell, 1977. Named an outstanding science book by a joint committee of the National Science Teachers Association and the Children's Book Council.

Patent, Dorothy Hinshaw. *The World of Worms.* New York: Holiday House, 1978. Provides useful information for adults.

Pringle, Lawrence. *Into the Woods: Exploring the Forest Ecosystem.* New York: Macmillan, 1973. Excellent.

Scott, John M. *Senses: Seeing, Hearing, Tasting, Touching & Smelling.* New York: Parents Magazine Press, 1975. Grades 2 to 4.

Selsam, Millicent E. *Play with Seeds.* New York: William Morrow, 1957.

Tallarice, Tony. *Metric Man Activity Book.* New York: Grossett & Dunlap, 1977. A paperback.

Walther, Tom. *A Spider Might.* San Francisco/New York: Sierra Club Books/Scribner, 1978. Delightful for reading aloud to a child.

White, William Jr., and Sara Jane White. *A Terrarium in Your Home.* New York: Sterling, 1976. For adults.

Zim, Herbert S., and Clarence Cottam. *Insects.* New York: Golden Press, 1951. One of the Golden Nature Guides; other books in this series are also suitable for both adults and children.

Index